Don't Stress

How to Handle Life's Little Problems

Helaine Becker

Scholastic Canada Ltd.
Toronto New York London Auckland Sydney
Mexico City New Delhi Hong Kong Buenos Aires

Scholastic Canada Ltd.
604 King Street West, Toronto, Ontario M5V 1E1, Canada

Scholastic Inc.
557 Broadway, New York, NY 10012, USA

Scholastic Australia Pty Limited
PO Box 579, Gosford, NSW 2250, Australia

Scholastic New Zealand Limited
Private Bag 94407, Botany, Manukau 2163, New Zealand

Scholastic Children's Books
Euston House, 24 Eversholt Street, London NW1 1DB, UK

www.scholastic.ca

Library and Archives Canada Cataloguing in Publication
Becker, Helaine, 1961-, author
        Don't stress : how to handle life's little problems / Helaine Becker.
ISBN 978-1-4431-4842-9 (paperback)
        1. Stress in children--Juvenile literature. 2. Stress (Psychology)--
Juvenile literature. I. Title.
BF723.S75B43 2016   j155.4'189042   C2015-908021-5

Photo credits:
Cover: Rainbow and clouds Shutterstock © Hluboki Dzianis
Hot air balloons in sky Shutterstock © Keng Merry Mikey Melody
Interiors: Page 33 by Simon Kwan © Scholastic Canada Ltd.; all others
Shutterstock.com.

10 9 8 7 6   Printed in Canada 121   18 19 20 21 22

MIX
Paper from
responsible sources
FSC® C004071

Table of Contents

Introduction

It's no secret that kids experience stress as much as adults. You've got responsibilities — like getting to school on time, doing homework or performing chores at home. And sometimes relationships — with friends, with family, with classmates — don't go 100 percent smoothly. This can cause stress too.

It's no secret, either, that most kids don't have a lot of control over how they spend their time. You don't get to decide what time school starts or what homework you are assigned or what's for dinner. No wonder you feel overwhelmed now and then.

This book contains dozens of tips for dealing with stress! It will also help you recognize what kinds of things cause you aggravation so you can manage your reactions, keep calm and carry on.

Not every suggestion will strike a chord with you immediately. That's because no two kids, or two situations, will be exactly alike. But chances are that at least a few of the ideas here will do the trick and help you coast through the situations kids say are the most stressful.

So turn on some tunes (page 74), curl up with a good book (this one!) and relax!

S-T-R-E-T-C-H

Your muscles have been working hard all day. Say "Thank you!" with a nice, long stretch.

When you stretch, it's like giving a mini-massage to your muscles. Blood flows into them, making them feel toasty warm. Stretching also loosens up and relaxes too-tight muscle fibres. That makes the rest of you feel more relaxed too.

Spend a few minutes stretching before bedtime. You'll sleep like a baby.

Neck Stretch

Gaze forward. Slowly bring your right ear to your right shoulder. Repeat on the other side.

Shoulder and Back Stretch

Kneel on the floor with the tops of your feet flat on the floor, the soles of your feet facing up. Sit on your heels. Gently bend forward at the waist and rest your torso between your thighs, lowering your forehead toward the floor. Let your arms drop down in whatever position feels most comfortable for you — reaching forward, at your sides or open wide. Hold this position, breathing in and out for three to five breaths.

Hold each stretch
for about 30-60 seconds.
Keep it gentle. Stretching should
feel good, not hurt. And remember
to keep breathing throughout
the stretch!

Arm and Side Stretch

Standing comfortably, put your arms straight
out in front. Lace your fingers together, palms
toward you, and raise your arms above your
head. Feel the stretch in your arms.

Now turn your palms up toward the sky and
stretch again (this stretches a few more,
different muscles). With hands still joined, gently
bend to the right from your waist and hold the
stretch. Straighten up, then bend gently to the
left.

Hand and Wrist Stretch

Sit comfortably and let your arms drop to your
sides. Shake your hands toward the ground.
Wiggle your fingers and rotate your wrists.
Then raise your hands up in front of you and
shake, wiggle and rotate them again.

Next hold your right arm straight out in front
of you, fingers extended, palm down. Keep your
elbow straight and use your left hand to gently
bend your wrist, pulling your right hand back
toward your body, so your fingers are pointing
up. Hold this stretch for 10 to 20 seconds. Then

fold your right hand down, fingers pointing down, and hold. Repeat this stretch on the other side.

Finish the stretching session by gently massaging each hand, one at a time. Do each finger individually. Don't forget to massage the palms of your hands and the spaces between the fingers too! Give both hands another shake to shake off stress completely.

Children smile more than adults — about 400 times a day, on average.

Smile

When you smile (even when you fake it), your brain receives an I'm-smiling-so-I-must-be-happy message. Sure enough, a few minutes later, your mood lifts and you're humming a happy tune.

Chances are when you smile at someone, they'll smile back at you! That will also lighten your mood.

Practise this breathing technique when you are relaxed and you'll be all set to use it when you need it.

Breathe

Breathing is one of the most important things you do every day. You literally can't live without it! When you take deeper than normal breaths, it increases the amount of oxygen your cells receive. That gives you more energy. It also stretches the muscles in your chest and massages the organs in your abdomen. That helps your body function better.

Deep, long breaths also send an "all clear" signal to your brain and body, telling them everything is okay and you can relax.

If you're feeling stressed, you can feel calmer by taking "all clear" breaths.

Start by placing one hand on your belly and one on your upper chest. Inhale through your nose. Let the air flow deep into the lower part of your lungs. You will feel your belly rise under your hand. Your upper chest will remain relatively still.

Breathe in for a count of 1, 2, 3.

Then exhale through your mouth for another count of 1, 2, 3. Feel your belly sink under your hand.

Repeat five to ten times or until you start to feel calmer.

Colourful mandalas — ornate, circular patterns — have been used as meditation aids for thousands of years. They also make great designs for colouring.

Colour

There's something tremendously soothing about filling clear, clean areas with brilliant colour and watching a beautiful picture emerge out of it. That might be one reason why adult colouring books have become all the rage!

But why should adults have all the fun? You can chill too, just by getting out your colouring markers and spending a few minutes engaged in colour therapy.

On your own?
Tell your alternate version of
events to your journal. Exaggerate!
Add goofy doodles and — GRRRR!
CHOMP! SPLAT! —
silly sound effects.

Spin It

So the dog really *did* eat your homework.
Look on the bright side: you now possess a
packet of comic gold — priceless material you
can spin into a side-splittingly hilarious story.

Act out what happened for your friends. Ramp
up the fun factor with crazy gestures, canine
sounds and other doggy-dramatic effects.
You'll have your pals — and you too! —
laughing in no time.

Daydream

Do you imagine yourself winning an Olympic medal, accepting an Academy Award or saving the day as a superhero?

It's fun to daydream. It also happens to be an A–1 stressbuster. Imagining pleasant events can help you solve problems and figure out life goals. It improves your mood and helps you sleep better at night. And it also provides a temporary escape from stressful or unpleasant experiences.

So let your mind wander now and then. (Just not while your teacher is explaining a new math concept!)

Count to Ten

About to lose your cool? Count slowly and silently to ten before you react.

This mini time-out gives your brain time to catch up with your emotions. That makes you feel calmer. It also helps you make better decisions. Count on it!

"Grow" your own blooms by drawing some cartoony flowers on cardboard. Cut them out and place in a kooky container for instant colour. The extra upside: cartoon-a-blooms last forever!

Arrange Some Flowers

Set a single sprig of lily of the valley in an elegant blue vase. Or arrange an armload of starry purple asters, gathered from the roadside, in an old-fashioned pitcher.

Whatever your style, whatever the season, flowers are always in fashion. And of course they smell fabulous! No wonder a cheerful bouquet — especially one you arranged yourself — is sure to put a smile on your face.

Stay in the Moment

Let the past stay in the past. Focus instead on the here and now.

Try it right now! Pay careful attention to what's going on around you. What can you see? What can you smell? Feel? Hear?

By concentrating on what's happening now, you free yourself to create a happier and more relaxed future.

Meditate

Everybody needs some quiet time now and then. Meditating — engaging in quiet thought or contemplation — is a great way to get it and make the most of it! And it's probably something you already do, at least occasionally!

When you meditate for relaxation, your aim is to consciously quiet your mind. When you first start out, it can be hard to do. Your brain is a very busy, very active and very noisy place! But over time you'll find it gets easier and easier to do. And a quieter mind is a calmer one.

Find a cozy place where you won't be disturbed. Get comfy. Close your eyes. Try not to think about anything other than the sound and feel of your own breath moving in and out of your lungs. When a thought flits through your mind, let it go. Mentally "put it on a shelf" and leave it there. Some people find it helpful to focus on a repeated word, sound or image while meditating. These techniques seem to keep distracting thoughts at bay.

When you're ready, open your eyes and stretch.

You've just meditated!

Make a To-Do List

RRRRING! Your alarm rings and you scramble out of bed, already in a rush. There's so much to do this morning: feed the dog, remember the permission slip for the field trip and pack that math set you worked so hard on! No wonder you sometimes forget something. And that makes you feel — *ACK!*

Making a to-do list takes the *ACK!* out of keeping track. Jot down each task as you think of it. Check each one off as you complete it.

Have a Healthy Snack

Feeling tense? Irritable? Snappish? Maybe you're out of sorts because you're out of gas.

Take some time to refill your tank with a healthy snack. You're bound to feel more upbeat after you've chowed down.

Avoid snacks that include a lot of added sugar or salt, large portions of fried or other high-fat foods (small portions are okay) and foods that are highly processed.

Take a Break

You've been working all evening on your book report, but you're only halfway through! And you're running out of time! What to do?

Take a break. Yes, really. Get up, walk around, stretch your arms, your legs, your neck.

When you return to that book report, you'll have renewed energy and focus. You'll get more done in less time and feel less stressed too.

Break It Down

Does a big project leave you feeling overwhelmed? Break it down into smaller chunks.

For starters, make a list of steps you'll need to follow to finish the project. Then set target dates for completing each task. For example:

1. Research Jurassic Era dinosaurs.
2. Choose five species and list their traits and other interesting facts about them.
3. Write a paragraph about each one.
4. Write introduction and conclusion.
5. Proofread.
6. Done!

In this way, your ginormous Jurassic project gets broken up into bite-sized bits. So much easier to swallow!

A warm shower can be just as soothing as a bath. For extra oomph, position the shower nozzle so the spray massages tight muscles in your neck or shoulders.

Take a Warm Bath

Fill the tub with warm water. Test the temperature by holding your hand under the tap as it runs — you want the water to be comfortably warm, but not scalding hot!

Try a little aromatherapy! Add a few drops of scented essential oil to the water (use sparingly for best results). Your sweetly scented bath may help you to de-stress. The smell of lavender oil, for example, can be particularly relaxing.

Slip into the water and . . . *ahhh*.

Follow up a lovely, warm bath by putting on some body lotion. Your skin will gratefully drink up the added moisture as you give yourself a gentle, relaxing massage.

Practise a Sport

Engaging in a sport you love, even for a few minutes, will help take your mind off your problems. That gives you an important mental break. The physical exercise will also stimulate your brain to release endorphins — neurochemicals that relieve stress and make you feel happier.

As you boost your sports skills, you'll undoubtedly get a boost in self-esteem, which is also a proven stress-buster.

So whenever you feel hot under the collar, spend a few minutes practising your favourite sport. It's a gold-medal way to regain your cool.

> Putting a problem into words helps you define exactly what the real issue is. That makes it easier to solve.

Ask for Advice

Sometimes the best solution to a problem is also the simplest: ask for advice.

You're probably not the first person in the world to have had this particular problem! A friend, teacher or family member might have the answer right at her fingertips. Or she might help you come up with a new solution.

Ask more than one person for ideas. If they all offer the same advice, you can be pretty sure it's worth following.

Is every suggestion different? That will tell you there isn't one right answer. With a range of ideas to choose from, you're free to pick ones that work best for you.

Take a Nap

Curl up on the sofa with a cozy blanket. Stretch out on the grass in the shade beneath a tree. Or lower the blinds and tuck yourself into bed with your favourite stuffed animal.

A catnap is like a mini vacation for your brain and body. You'll wake up feeling like the cat's meow!

Here are some tips for better napping:

- The best time for a nap is late afternoon.
- A short nap (10–20 minutes) can make you feel more energized. A longer nap (60–90 minutes) can boost creativity and problem-solving skills. Naps can also improve your memory and make it easier to learn new things.
- Napping lying down is better than napping in a chair, no matter how comfy the chair.
- The darker the room, the better the nap.

Put Your Feet Up

When your world feels upside down, one way to help set it right is to turn *yourself* upside down.

Lie on your back with your feet up on a chair or your legs extended against a wall. After a few minutes, you may start to feel calmer and steadier.

Why does this position feel so soothing? Many people think by raising your legs above your head, you stimulate the parasympathetic nervous system — the system that signals your body to rest and digest. Others think that it's just a pleasant way to give yourself a well-deserved break.

Listen to the people in your life. Listen to their words, but also to the *sound* of their voices. What does their tone tell you about what they are feeling? When you become a good listener, you avoid misunderstandings. You feel closer to people, and they feel closer to you too!

Listen

Sounds fill your world: funny sounds, exciting sounds, ordinary sounds. They all carry information. Take a few moments to listen to them — to really, really listen. You may be surprised by what you hear. You may be surprised by what you learn.

When you focus on listening to the sounds around you, you stop focussing, if even for a moment, on yourself. Careful listening also helps you to concentrate on the here and now, which is a proven stress-beater.

Practise Gratitude

There are many ways to practise gratitude.

Keep a gratitude journal. Write down one thing you can be grateful for every day. It will help you focus on the good things that happen in your life. And if one day you are feeling low, you'll be able to reread your previous days' entries and remind yourself of all the good things you had forgotten!

Pledge not to gripe, whine or complain. Use the energy you save to find or do something more positive.

Give a compliment at least once a day.

Share a pleasant observation or opinion with someone else. They may be grateful to you for pointing it out!

Take a few moments every day to *notice* and *appreciate* the good in your life.

Sleep on It

You've been wrestling with a thorny problem all day and you're still no closer to the answer! So sleep on it. When you wake up in the morning, the answer might be plain as day.

Still feel fogged in? No worries. Your good night's sleep will help you approach the problem with fresh eyes and renewed energy.

Say "I Care About You!"

Are there people in your life who matter a lot to you? Who you'd miss terribly if they weren't a part of your life?

Tell them. They'll feel wonderful! And so will you.

Here's how:

- Do something special for them.
- Express your feelings in a poem or a drawing that you created just for them.
- Write it in a card or an email, or even on a sticky note.
- Send them a gift.
- Give them a hug.

Look for opportunities to give a compliment. It helps you focus on people's strengths, not their weaknesses. It also helps you learn to recognize — and honour — your own strengths.

Give a Compliment

Did you see the way she kicked the soccer ball? It was a perfect pass! And his presentation on the Incas was incredible! You learned so much!

A compliment is one of the easiest things to give.

"You have the best laugh ever!"

"That's such a beautiful drawing."

"I liked your speech."

"That colour looks great on you."

The best compliments are ones that come from the heart. A sincere compliment will always make the other person feel special and appreciated.

Take a Compliment

Sometimes getting a compliment feels awkward.

It's tempting to shrug the compliment off. ("Anyone could have done it.") Or explain why the compliment isn't deserved. ("It was just a fluke. I didn't even know where Jenny was when I kicked the ball toward the goal!")

Resist the temptation. When you deflect a compliment, you do two things:

1. You do a disservice to yourself.
2. You deny the other person a chance to give a sincere compliment and invalidate her opinion.

Instead, acknowledge the kind words with a simple "Thank you."

32

Weigh the Pros and Cons

Life is full of choices, and it's not always clear what path to take.

Setting out the advantages and disadvantages of any course of action helps you make a better decision. One way to do this, especially when your choice is between two clear options, is to create a list of pros and cons.

Write your question on a sheet of paper. Beneath it, create two columns. In one column, list all the good reasons — the pros — to take a certain path. In the other, put all the reasons why you shouldn't — the cons. Compare the two columns.

You may notice the advantages of saying YES clearly outweigh the disadvantages, or vice versa.

And if they are more evenly matched, that's okay too. You've learned there isn't one right answer. You can feel more confident and less stressed about whichever decision you make.

Should I join the
swim team?

PROS	CONS
Lots of fun	Takes a lot of time
Make new friends	Hate getting up in the morning (and practice is every day before school!)
Get plenty of exercise	Might interfere with keeping my grades up

Try Progressive Relaxation

This easy technique is a great way to feel more relaxed fast!

Find a quiet place where you can sit comfortably and won't be disturbed. Close your eyes.

Focus your mental attention on your left foot. Curl your toes, tensing the muscles tight, tight, tight for about five seconds. Then let them go limp. Tense the muscles again — tight, tight, tight — for another five seconds. Let them relax.

Take a few moments — about fifteen seconds — to notice how soft and heavy your foot now feels. Next, do the same thing with the other foot.

Now tense your foot AND the muscles in the lower part of your left leg. Repeat as before. Then switch legs and repeat the process on the right.

Continue tensing and relaxing the different muscles in your body, moving from one section of the body to the next.

When you have progressed through all the muscles of your body, take a moment to note how you feel. A bit lighter and looser, no?

Follow this sequence:

- Left foot
- Right foot
- Left foot and lower leg
- Right foot and lower leg
- Entire left leg
- Entire right leg
- Left hand (clench your fist)
- Left hand and arm
- Right hand
- Right hand and arm
- Buttocks
- Belly (suck it in)
- Chest (breathe in deeply)
- Back (squeeze your shoulder blades together)
- Neck
- Shoulders (shrug them up to your ears)
- Mouth (open your mouth WIDE)
- Eyes (squeeze your eyelids tightly shut)
- Forehead (raise your eyebrows, then furrow them)

Play a Musical Instrument

You don't need to be a concert violinist to make a joyful noise. Bang out "Twinkle, Twinkle, Little Star" on a toy piano. Fill some glasses with water and tap out a tune with a spoon. Shake, shake, shake boxes of pasta — and shake, shake, shake your hips in time with your riotous rigatoni rhythm.

Any way you do it, making music makes you feel good and gives you the chance to express yourself. But that's not all. When you hear the music you make, your brain releases dopamine. This is a chemical that gives you feelings of pleasure and satisfaction.

Jump for Joy

When you need a lift, lift your body. Jump!

Try:

- Jumping rope
- Doing twenty jumping jacks
- Jumping on a trampoline

39

Write in a Journal

Your journal is all yours and yours alone —
perfectly private. In it, you can say whatever you
think, whatever you feel. Journal writing helps
you get it off your chest (whatever *it* is!), get it
out of your system and get a fresh perspective.

A journal doesn't need to be fancy. It can be
as simple as a stack of loose-leaf paper kept
in a binder, or an old notebook that you've
decorated in a way you like.

You can write in it every day or only when the
spirit moves you. It's entirely up to you. Either
way, keeping a journal is a great way to clear
your mind.

> Gossip hurts three people: the person being talked about, the person telling the tale and the listener.

Skip the Gossip

It's no fun to be gossiped about, of course. But even the kids who do the gossiping feel stressed. And with good reason: we know that friends who are happy to dish *to* us will just as gladly dish *about* us.

So skip the gossip game. Here's how:

- Don't be the one spreading the rumours. While it might feel exciting to share a piece of juicy gossip, you'll get a reputation as being someone who can't be trusted.
- If someone else is doing the dishing, cut it off by saying you're not interested or walk away.
- Choose to hang with friends who talk about ideas, not other people.

Going to sleep at the same time every night — and getting up at around the same time every morning, even on weekends — is another way to keep yourself on an even keel.

Stick to a Routine

Chill time at 4

Homework at 5

Dinner at 6

Piano practice at 7:00

Bath at 8

Book and bed at 8:30

Lights out! 9:00

At first glance, having a predictable, daily routine like this might seem ho-hum. It's anything but! Routines can help you feel grounded. They can save you time. And with fewer decisions to make every day, you reserve your precious brain power for the really important ones!

> "Hard times require furious dancing."
> — Alice Walker

Have a Dance Party

Get the better of a blah mood by getting your personal party started! Just blast your favourite tunes and bust out some soul-stirring moves. (Mirror ball optional.)

43

Spin Like a Helicopter

Remember when you were a little kid and you used to throw your arms out wide, then spin, spin, spin like a helicopter? It felt *soooo* good! You would spin until you couldn't spin any longer, then fall to the ground and feel the world seem to spin around *you*.

You don't need to be a little kid to "helicopter." Recapture that fab feeling of abandon by going for a spin right now.

Does the
word STRESSED
give you stress? Just read
the word backwards. Now
it says DESSERTS!

Change Your Perspective

What do you see in this picture?

Some people see a vase. Some see two faces. Both are right. It just depends on how you look at it!

It's the same thing with problems: you can get stuck seeing them in one way. But change up your point of view and the same situation can suddenly look completely different.

45

Take a Walk

When you take a walk, you don't need to have a destination. Just getting outside and stretching your legs feels good.

Start out fast. Take long, quick strides. Let your arms swing freely. Get that blood pumping.

After a few minutes, slow your pace. Look up at the sky. Pay attention to what's happening around you. What do you hear? What do you smell? What's *different* from the last time you walked along this route?

You can
turn almost any activity
into a game. Need to tidy your room?
Assign points for every item you put
away. When you reach a predetermined
goal, you win! (Don't forget to give
yourself style points for
folding with flair.)

Play a Game

It can take two minutes (Tic-Tac-Toe) or all day
(Monopoly).

It can be something you play on your own
(Solitaire) or something you play with someone
else (Tag).

You can play a game with pencil and paper
(Hangman), a ball (HORSE) or a console
(Minecraft).

You can play with a baby (Peekaboo!) or even a
pet (Fetch!).

Whatever game you play, you'll win big at
reducing stress.

The Soothing Power of Water

Have you ever noticed that beautiful gardens almost always have some kind of water feature — a lovely fountain, or even a simple birdbath? That's because water tends to make people feel calm and at peace.

If you are lucky enough to live near water, spend time enjoying it. Walk along the shore, your toes digging into the sand. Or follow the river trail and watch as a stick you toss into the current disappears from sight. You'll feel your troubles float away too.

You can get a water fix even if there's no lake at your doorstep:

- Download some audio of waves crashing on a beach, or raindrops plinking on a tin roof.
- Visit a community pool for a refreshing dog paddle.
- Set up an inexpensive tabletop fountain and bring the beautiful burble of water indoors.
- Get out your rubber ducky and get into the bath.

Draw Something

Do you have trouble putting your feelings into words sometimes? Try drawing them. You don't need to have any special talent for drawing. You don't need fancy materials either. You just need to give yourself permission to draw whatever comes to mind.

Drawing forces your eyes and hand to work together in a pleasant, repetitive rhythm. That helps soothe your nervous system. When you focus on the details of your drawing, it also helps shut out, and shut off, the distracting chatter in your head. You wind up living more fully in the moment. That's calming too.

When you draw, whatever you draw, your subconscious gets a chance to express itself. You'll feel better after you get whatever's troubling you off your chest and onto paper.

If negative self-talk keeps getting you down, arm yourself against it by writing three things you like about yourself on a slip of paper. Keep it with you and look at it whenever the negative self-talk starts up.

Say Yes to Positive Self-Talk

Self-talk is the little voice in your head that chatters all day long. Many times it's a downer: "I'm not good at sports." "They're going to laugh at me." "I'm going to fail that test." Without even realizing it, you've become your own worst enemy.

When you hear that niggling voice in your head putting you down, ask yourself, "Is what I'm telling myself true?" (It probably isn't!) Then reply with some positive self-talk. ("I'm bright and hard-working. I studied, so I'm prepared. I will do fine on the test.")

You'll feel better right away, and with a more realistic attitude, you'll be more likely to succeed at whatever you try too!

Pay It Forward

Instead of simply paying someone *back* for doing you a favour, pay it *forward* by doing something nice for someone else.

When you pay it forward, one kind act can go a long way. Like ripples in water, it spreads. From person to person, from place to place, each good deed you do gets magnified.

51

Just Do It!

Do you tend to put off doing tasks you don't enjoy? That might seem like a good idea at first, but procrastination creates its own problems. You may wind up having to rush to get your job done. Or you may even — oops! — forget to do it altogether. Now you're in hot water!

One thing is certain: procrastination is bound to bump up your stress level.

Try these tips for beating back the procrastination beast and buying yourself some well-deserved breathing space:

- Just do it. You may find once you begin, the rest of the job flows easily. Before you know it, you're finished!

- Set yourself a firm deadline for when you will start the task, and when you will finish it. Then stick to it.

- Do the easy parts first. Getting a real accomplishment under your belt will make the more challenging parts of the job seem more manageable.

- Remind yourself of the benefits you will enjoy when you finish the task. That will help motivate you to get cracking.

- Don't worry that you won't do the job "perfectly." There is no such thing as perfect. A completed job is far better than one that remains undone.

Remember: you may *admire* a flawless marble sculpture, but you *love* your soft, ratty old teddy bear.

Celebrate Imperfection

Nobody's perfect. Yet a lot of us imagine that we should be, and then we beat ourselves up when we don't meet our own unrealistic expectations.

Don't waste your energy trying to be perfect. Instead, celebrate *imperfection*. Your quirks are what make you unique. They are also what make you lovable.

Let Molehills Stay Molehills

Do you let small problems grow and grow and GROW in your mind until they seem like insurmountable obstacles? People call this habit "making mountains out of molehills." Even small obstacles can trip you up because you imagine them to be much larger than they really are.

When you find yourself imagining a problem is too big to handle, hold up your hand like you are saying "STOP!" What does your hand block from your view? The chair on the other side of the room? The tree in the distance? A problem is like that chair or tree. No matter how big it is, you have the power to cut it right back down to a size smaller than your hand. It's all a matter of perspective.

Open a Worry Window

Do you spend a lot of time worrying? Make a new rule for yourself, one that will limit the time you spend fretting to a specific, short time period or "worry window." (Late afternoon is a good time for a worry window. Close to bedtime, not so much.)

If you catch yourself worrying at another time of day, tell yourself, "I will think about this during my worry window." Write it down and promise yourself you will deal with it later. Then actively turn your mind to something else. With practice you will get better and better at postponing your worry time and better at learning how to take control of your thoughts so they don't control you.

Leave Your Worries at the Door

Place a basket inside your front door where you can put your keys, backpack, etc., when you come in. Drop your worries into it too! This simple practice sends a message to your brain that you've reached a place of refuge and can now — *ahhh* — relax.

Make a Worry List

During your worry window, make a list of the things you are worrying about. Put them in order from most worrying to least worrying. Seeing them on paper seems to have a way of cutting them down to size.

When you review your list, you may realize the worries that seemed so distressing at lunchtime just don't seem to bother you any longer. That is a useful reminder that worries come and go and shouldn't be allowed to ruin your day.

Have a Brainstorm

When we worry, we go over and over a problem in our minds. We imagine all the worst things that can happen! That becomes a habit.

Instead, take a hard look at the worry ("I'm going to fail the test!"). Is there a concrete action you can take to change the situation and solve the problem? ("I can set up a study schedule and stick to it!")

Brainstorm solutions to as many of the problems on your worry list as you can. If you're stuck, get input from friends, family members or your teachers. With an action plan in hand, you can cross those worries off the list — permanently.

Accept Uncertainty

A lot of worries revolve around imaginary what-ifs. What if there is a zombie apocalypse? What if I tell a joke at the lunch table and no one laughs? What if I get lost on my first day of middle school?

This kind of worry can't be cut down to size by coming up with an action plan. Instead, the trick is to accept that you can't control everything in your life. But you *can* trust that you and the people in your life will be able to deal with the problem successfully *if and when it actually happens.*

If, for example, you worry that you won't be able to find your way around your new school, recognize that you will be able to sort out what to do *at the time.* You could ask another student or a teacher to point out the way to the caf. So there's no need for worrying today about a what-if you will be able to solve when the time comes.

Give Up Control

You're growing up, and as you do, you become more and more responsible for yourself and your actions. Maybe you are now in charge of making and packing your lunch instead of having it made for you.

But no matter how grown up you are, you never become responsible for *everything*. (You may have to pack that lunch, but you don't have to grow the ingredients!)

Even so, some people feel and act as if they are responsible for everything. That's a lot of pressure and can lead to frustration when things don't go as planned.

You can't control everything. It simply can't be done. In life, some things are uncertain, and it isn't your job to change that.

When you're out in nature, take a notebook to record your thoughts or draw a sketch of something you see: a dramatic sunset, an oddly angled branch that looks like a nose. When you can't get outdoors, flip through your notebook for a nature fix.

Experience Nature

Spending time in the natural world has long been a way to soothe the soul. Studies suggest that getting out in nature can actually change the way blood flows in your brain. It flows less to areas associated with brooding and negative thoughts. That helps take your mind off your problems, which makes you feel more at peace.

Watch a dragonfly swoop across a meadow or a maple key swirl and spin through the air. Take a deep breath of pine-scented air as you hike through a forest. Or examine the way a dandelion's yellow petals nestle tightly against each other, like tiles on a roof. Even in the heart of the city, nature shows itself — an aster growing from a crack in the sidewalk, a snowbank glistening in the moonlight. Look for it.

Bring Nature Indoors

Bring nature indoors by setting up a windowsill garden. The plants don't just look nice, they also help you feel good! They release oxygen and help to clear the air of carbon dioxide. That helps your body work better. They also smell great and look beautiful. Simply looking at them and inhaling their perfumes can lift your mood.

Taking care of your plants is a stress-reliever too. It gives you a break from routine tasks and helps distract you from other niggling worries.

Go Wild

Spend some time with an animal. Take a dog for a walk, romp with a kitten or feed a fish.

Passing time with animals is a doggone great way to relieve stress.

Don't have a pet?

- Visit a pet store.
- Offer to walk a neighbour's dog.
- Check out a zoo or aquarium.
- Listen to the birds in the park.
- Offer to help care for the animals at a local farm or animal shelter.

Try Something New

If you're feeling stressed, the last thing you should do is take on a new challenge, right? Not always.

Sometimes, trying something new is *exactly* what you need. When you take a risk, you'll feel more excited and engaged. You'll undoubtedly learn something new, which will help you feel more confident and capable. You'll gain a new perspective.

So go for it!

Wipe the Slate Clean

Each morning you wake up to a new day, a fresh start, a clean slate. Or do you? Do you carry over worries, frustrations or disappointments from the day before?

Leave yesterday in the past.

When you get into bed at night, imagine the day as a page in a scrapbook. Look at the things you did, the experiences you had during the day, and decide which ones to keep and which ones to toss out.

Paste the "keepers" onto your mental scrapbook page. Then turn the page, leaving a fresh, clean one ready for the next day.

Learn from Your Mistakes

Everybody makes mistakes. It's an important part of learning and growing. It's how you deal with mistakes that makes a difference.

Do you cringe when you think about something you messed up, and then promise yourself never, *ever*, ever to think about it again? Or do you think about what you could do better next time? In other words, do you use your mistakes as a way to learn and improve?

A mistake is a door to discovery. It's only a mistake if you don't learn from it.

DO Sweat It!

Go for a run. Take a vigorous spin on your bike. Skate. Swim. Pump iron. Dance. It doesn't matter how you do it, just do it. Work up a *serious* sweat.

Getting sweaty is one of the best ways to beat stress. When you're huffing and puffing, focussing on making it to the next landmark or getting into position for your shot on goal, you can't think about anything else! Vigorous exercise provides a welcome way to clear your mind.

Aerobic exercises reduce the levels of cortisol, a stress-related hormone, in your body. And a cardio workout releases chemicals in your brain called endorphins that make you feel happier and more relaxed. Exercise also burns off nervous energy that could otherwise leave you tense and fretful. After a sweat session, you'll feel tired but relaxed. So *do* sweat it!

Feeling artistic?
Decorate your worry stone
by drawing an interesting pattern or
meaningful word on it with a marker.
Or make your own worry "stone" using
air-drying clay. Mould it into a shape
that is the perfect fit for you!

Find a Worry Stone

Next time you're out for a walk, scan the ground for stones. Look for one that's small and smooth and feels nice in your hand.

Slip the stone in your pocket. Keep it with you during the day. When you feel tense or nervous, touch the stone in your pocket. Let its familiar weight and shape ground you. Let its smooth shape help smooth away your cares.

Make Your Own Stress Ball

Fiddling with a soft, squishy "stress ball" is a simple way to help relieve stress.

You will need:

> 1 to 2 cups (250–500 ml) sand or flour
>
> 2 plastic zipper bags
>
> 1 small cotton sock
>
> duct tape

1. Scoop the sand or flour into one plastic zipper bag until it's the size you want. Seal it.
2. Slip the filled bag into the second bag. Seal it.
3. Tape over the bag's seal with the duct tape. This will help prevent sand from leaking out.
4. Slip the filled bag into the toe of the sock.
5. Tie a firm knot in the sock to keep the bag in place. Turn over the extra fabric to make a sleeve over the knot and ball.
6. Decorate any way you like.
7. Squeeze.

Make a Worry Jar

Is there something on your mind you can't seem to stop thinking about? Put a worry jar to use!

Write your worry on a slip of paper, then put the slip in the jar and seal the lid.

Now let the jar hold on to that worry for you while you go off and do something else. You can come back to it during your worry window (p. 56).

Don't forget to take a break. You don't have to be doing something all the time. Sometimes it's enough to just *be*.

Give Yourself a Break

Don't be too hard on yourself. Sure, you want to do your best. But you won't always be at your best. Cut yourself some slack. So what if you didn't do that thing, whatever it is, exactly 100 percent perfectly! Will it matter next week? Next month? One hundred years from now?

What would you say to a friend who was beating herself up over a mistake she'd made? Would you say, "Forget it. Let it go. Move on. I like you anyway."? Then tell yourself the same thing.

Plan Something Fun

Arrange a movie marathon with a bunch of friends. Organize an outing to the zoo. Corral the gang for a Saturday morning game of touch football at the park. When you plan something fun and make it happen, you win in three ways:

1. You enjoy anticipating the fun you will have.
2. You take your mind off other things.
3. You have a great time!

Talking to someone is more effective than texting for relieving stress and building relationships.

Share Your Feelings

There's something liberating about sharing your feelings. Saying how you feel out loud makes uncomfortable emotions like "I'm scared" or "I'm confused" easier to deal with. And sharing joyful emotions like "I'm so excited" or "I feel so proud of myself!" doubles the delight.

What if you feel like sharing and no one's around? Tell a teddy bear. Or a tree. Or better yet, pick up the phone.

Singing releases endorphins and oxytocin, brain chemicals that make you feel terrific! It's also wonderful aerobic exercise.

Sing!

You can do it in the shower or as part of a choir. It doesn't matter how or where you sing, but belting out a tune is a sure-fire way to lift your spirits. Don't worry about how it sounds. Most of us will never be opera stars. But so what? Sing for your *own* pleasure.

Change How
You React

Toss a potato and an egg into a pot of boiling water. The water will harden the egg, but it will soften the potato.

You, happily, are neither an egg or a potato. You can choose how you will react to external events. Imagine, for example, that the picnic you were looking forward to gets rained out. You can spend the day moping. Or you can resolve to have fun anyway, and host an indoor picnic for your pals.

MUSIC = MAGIC.
It's so powerful, no one
can resist its spell.

Listen to Music

Turn on some tunes or put on the headphones. *POOF!* You've been transported.

You can use music to change your mood. If you feel low, for example, cue up some toe-tapping, finger-snapping tunes. You may find that your funk magically evaporates.

Or you can use music to *express* your mood. That's exactly why Blues music exists (and why it works so well)!

Some people experience flow more than others. Athletes and artists, for example, spend long, intense hours perfecting their skills. When they are in flow, they tend to perform best or create their best work.

Immerse Yourself in a Hobby You Love

Have you ever been deeply involved in a task then look up at the clock and realize *hours* have passed without you noticing?

When you are so absorbed in a task the world around you seems to disappear, that's called flow. And when you are experiencing flow, you feel more excited, engaged and happy than when you are not. Flow is the opposite of boredom.

To get in the flow:

1. Choose an activity that isn't too hard, or too easy. If it involves a bit of a stretch, that's good too.

2. Start with a clear goal. "I'm going to master this tricky piano piece in time for the recital."

3. Avoid interruptions. They yank you out of the flow state.

4. Enjoy each moment. One day, you'll look up and say, "*Eeep!* Where did the time go?" And you'll discover that not only have you met your goal, you've surpassed it.

Visualizing where
the event will take place can
be a big help. If you can, arrange to
visit the location where the event will
be held before the big day.

Picture It

It's only natural to be nervous when you tackle
something new and challenging. But pre-
performance jitters can be overcome with a
secret from the pros: visualization.

Visualization means you picture the activity
— like singing that solo on stage — in your
head, over and over again, before the big day.
Including as much detail as possible, you run
through the whole scene in your head, from
your first step on stage to your final encore. See
it all clearly: the way you phrase each line, how
you position your hands, the way you smile or
raise an eyebrow at the key moment in the song.

When you repeatedly picture yourself
succeeding in just this way, your chances of
knocking it out of the park soar.

Expect the Unexpected

It's a fact of life: sometimes things go wrong.

Whether you are getting ready for school on an ordinary Tuesday, or looking forward to your big day starring in the school show, there's a chance that something unexpected might happen to mess you up.

You don't have to let hiccups turn into personal disasters.

Brainstorm what some hiccups might be ahead of time, then make allowances for them. For example, do you have to present your team project at school first thing in the morning? Ask a family member to make sure you get up on time if your wonky alarm clock tends to malfunction.

A little advance preparation keeps hiccups manageable. If you expect the unexpected, you can also expect success!

Practice really does
make perfect.

Do the Work

One of the reasons we get nervous, especially before doing something new or challenging, is because we doubt whether we're up to the challenge. There's one sure-fire way to defeat that feeling: know your stuff cold.

Being totally on top of your subject will build your confidence and quell your nerves.

The harder you work at something, the easier it gets. And the easier it gets, the less stressful it is.

With plenty of advance preparation under your belt, you'll be more relaxed and confident. Which means you'll not only nail your performance, but you'll have a great time doing it.

Go with Your Gut

Do you ever get a mysterious, squiggly feeling in your stomach or an uncomfortable prickle at the back of your neck? They tell you something is wrong, but you can't put your finger on exactly what it is.

These physical sensations are signs that intuition is at work. Your *intuition* — or subconscious — notices all kinds of things your conscious mind might not. It works quickly too — much faster than the conscious mind can.

So trust it. Listening to your gut will help you make better decisions. It will help you avoid stressful situations *before* they become unmanageable.

Intuition can also tell you when something is right — like that you should sign up for the ski trip, or that the new kid in class is going to become your best friend for life. Listen to and follow those positive hunches too!

Create a Soothing Oasis

Everyone needs a place to chill, a place where you can be yourself, a place to just *be*.

Carve out a corner of your bedroom — or your whole bedroom, if you have one to yourself! — as a personal oasis. Decorate it with soothing colours. Keep it tidy — too much clutter or visual disorder tends to make people feel more anxious. Keep the lighting soft, the music low, the screens off. You'll be amazed by how quickly your stress evaporates whenever you enter your personal retreat.

Visit Another World

It's okay to get away — at least for a little while.

Curl up on the sofa with a swashbuckling adventure tale. Watch your favourite TV series. Draw a detailed map of the setting of your favourite movie — or of your own imaginary Flying Purple Pony Land. Build a giant Lego tower or out-of-this-world spaceship. Write a fan fiction story about your favourite character.

By taking a mini-vacation to an imaginary world, you get a break from the pressures of this one. Chances are you will return refreshed and renewed — and with a great story to tell too!

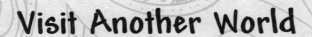

Do a Puzzle

Need a change of pace? Pull out a puzzle. Crossword, sudoku, Magic Maze, jigsaw — it doesn't matter what kind of puzzle you choose. While you're working on it, your mind will be (happily) preoccupied and too busy to think about other problems.

Go to Your Happy Place

Think about a place you really love, a place where you feel happy and safe. Or think about an object that makes you feel that way. People refer to images like these as a "happy place." When you picture your happy place in your mind, you may instantly feel calmer.

Why? Your brain can't always tell the difference between imagination and reality. If you picture something clearly enough, your brain reacts as if it's really happening. So if you picture something happy, you will feel happier. On the downside, if you picture upsetting scenes you will feel more upset.

Practise visualizing your happy place regularly. When you have one firmly in your mind, touch the tip of your left thumb to the tip of your left index finger and squeeze them together. Make this gesture every time you picture your happy place. Your brain will start to associate the finger squeeze with the calm and happy feeling.

In the future, when you need a quick boost, just squeeze those fingers together! You might find doing the finger-squeeze alone releases a flood of good feelings.

History Is Not Destiny

Maybe you've never been great at catching a baseball. Or perhaps your track record at track is less than stellar. But history is not destiny. In other words, the past does not determine the future. You do.

So give up statements like, "I'm no good at baseball," or "I'll never be a fast runner." They give the past more power than it deserves.

Instead, think about what you have to do to succeed at a particular activity. Practice tossing a ball against a wall and catching it a few hundred times to improve your fielding skills. Or add a daily run to your schedule to shave seconds off your race pace. Then do it, and take control of your future.

Have a Good Cry

When you weep you are helping your body rid itself of the hormones that contribute to your feelings of stress.

So have a good cry. You really will feel better afterwards!

Let It Out

Sometimes, you just feel like . . . *AAARGH!*

Go ahead. Let it out! Scream at the top of your lungs. Pound a pillow. Throw something. Have a good cry.

Letting out your emotions makes them easier to deal with. You may also feel calmer and clearer once your brain and body settle back down.

Strike a Power Pose

You probably know that your body language, how you sit or stand, can affect how others feel about you. But did you know it can also change how *you* feel?

Certain positions, like holding your arms up in a V over your head, make you feel more powerful or victorious. Other poses, like crossing your arms and bowing your head, make you feel small and weak.

Give yourself a boost by choosing power poses when you feel stressed. You can do this in private to bolster yourself before a tough test. Or you can consciously choose to assume one of the power poses in the midst of a nerve-wracking social situation.

Hold one of these power positions for two minutes. Do you feel more confident afterwards?

- Stand (or walk or jog) with your hands high in the air, like you're the first to cross the finish line.
- Lean back in a chair and cup the back of your neck in your clasped fingers. Stretch your legs out or put them up on a table.
- From a standing position, place both hands flat on a table and lean into them.
- Stand with your feet slightly apart and your hands on your hips. Keep your chin high too!
- Sit back, legs splayed, and your arms stretched out wide across the back of a sofa.

Next time you
are stumped, say,
"I don't know . . .
but I'll find out."

Say "I Don't Know"

It's hard to admit that you don't have *all* the
answers. And feeling out of the loop feels yucky.
So yucky, in fact, that many of us will go to
great lengths to avoid appearing ignorant. We'll
bluster, brag, waffle, even flat-out lie rather than
just own up and say "I don't know."

But when you *do* admit you don't know
something — *whew!* — you no longer need to
scramble or to cover, which leaves you free to
find out the answer and learn something new.

Most people won't think less of you for
admitting ignorance. Instead, they will respect
you for being honest and open. That, in
turn, will lead to better and less stressful
relationships.

Say "I'm Sorry"

Okay, you really *did* blow it. You made a big mistake or said something foolish or hurtful to a friend. You feel awful. But it's not too late to do something that could change everything. You can take a deep breath and apologize.

Apologizing can be hard. It's embarrassing to have to own up to a mistake. But by simply saying "I'm sorry," you instantly make the situation better.

An effective apology has four parts:

1. Say "I'm sorry."
2. Own up and admit it was your fault.
3. Ask how you can make things right.
4. Then do it!

Walk Away

Some groups or cliques aren't interested in including others. They let you know loud and clear: "No Admittance." They even enjoy the feeling of power they get from saying "No."

Accept the fact that the world includes petty tyrants like this, and that you don't need them.

So don't waste your time knocking at this particular gate. Turn around and go find new friends who will like you just the way you are.

Volunteer

The best way to stop fretting about your own stuff is to help someone else.

Volunteering takes you out of your head and distracts you from your everyday concerns. It helps put things in perspective. With more interesting things to think about than who-said-what-to-whom-in-the-caf-today, the problems that seemed insurmountable at noon seem trivial at six.

When you volunteer, you'll meet new people who care about the same things you do, and who may wind up becoming friends of the heart.

It feels good to do something useful. And it feels good to learn new things too, which will absolutely happen when you volunteer for a cause.

Last but not least, expect to earn yourself a big smile and a heartfelt "Thank you!" Those are two things that universally make us feel great.

Celebrate Failure

Wow! You really blew that. What an utter, colossal, mind-blowing failure it was. So get out the party favours. Toot the horns and toss the confetti. It's time to celebrate!

Failing is a necessary step of learning. Think of a baby, struggling to take his first steps and falling, over and over again. If he gave up the first time he fell down, he'd never learn to walk.

The more you fail, the more you learn.

So celebrate each and every failure. If you never fail, it's because you never took a risk. And if you don't take risks, you won't ever succeed. Failure + Failure = Success!

Take the Long View

Whenever you start working yourself up into a frenzy of anxiety about something, ask yourself, "Will this matter to me in a month? A year? Five years?"

Taking the long view can help keep the ordinary trials of everyday life in perspective. Chances are you won't even remember this particular issue a few weeks from now. And if you do, it might be with a laugh: "I can't believe I lost sleep over *that!*"

The times you feel least like reaching out to others are often the times you need it most.

Make Time for the Special People in Your Life

There's nothing like spending time with people you care about to put a bounce in your step and a smile on your face. But sometimes quality time with friends and family gets squeezed out by the pressures of a busy schedule. You keep meaning to hang out, but somehow the moment never comes. No wonder you feel stressed — and lonely.

Put "play dates" with the people you love at the very top of your to-do list. Write them in bold purple letters on your calendar. Then keep those dates!

It's Only an Opinion

Naysayers are everywhere. People who tell you all the reasons you can't, won't, shouldn't try something new. When someone tries to bring you down, remember this: It's only an opinion.

No one else holds secret knowledge about what you are or are not capable of. They only have their own opinions, their own thoughts and fears and biases. So consider their words — they may be telling you something you need to hear, like that you are unprepared for a particular task — but then make up your own mind.

People are entitled to their opinions, to be sure. But you are equally entitled to yours.

Jump In

Taking risks is scary. But that doesn't mean we
should avoid them altogether. In many cases, the
reward of trying something new far outweighs
the risk.

So go ahead — do it.

Join the party, the club, the sing-along in the caf.

Standing on the outside looking in is harder,
in the long run than taking a deep breath and
going for it. You'll be glad you took the chance.